Are You a MAMMAL?

by THOMAS KINGSLEY TROUPE

amicus LEARNING

illustrated by MARTINA ROTONDO

Randy was a rat. Yesterday, his neighbor said a strange word. "Those mammals are something else," Forrest the frog croaked.

"What's a mammal?" Randy asked.

"You don't want to know," Forrest said. Then he jumped into the swamp.

That was the problem. Randy DID want to know.

Randy set off to find mammals. He asked Beth the bird.

"A mammal? Not me. Most mammals are born alive. I hatched from an egg!"

“So, mammals don’t lay eggs?”
Randy made some notes.

“Most mammals don’t.
Just platypuses and echidnas.”

He found Fernando the fish.

"Are you kidding?
I'm not a mammal."

"Mammals feed their young milk!"
Randy wrote that down.

"What do you drink, water?"
Randy asked.

"Freshwater fish don't really need to!" Fernando cried.
"We live in the stuff!" He spit water at Randy.

He saw Sissy the snake slithering.

"No, *sssssir*."

"Mammals take care of their babies.
I leave my *eggsss* as *sssoon* as they're laid!"

"You don't keep your baby snakes safe?" Randy asked.

"My *kidsss* learn to *ssssurvive* on their own!"

Randy quickly added survival facts to his notes.

He saw Barry the beetle.

"Are you a mammal?" Randy asked.
"Afraid not, young chap," Barry replied.
"As you can see, I have no hair or fur upon my body."
"So, only mammals have fur and hair?" Randy asked.
"You are correct," Barry said.

Randy added hair and fur to his notebook.

Randy almost didn't see Lois the lizard.

"A mammal? Heavens no."

"Mammals are warm-blooded. Lizards are cold-blooded. We need the sun to stay warm."

“And a mammal’s body warms itself?” Randy asked.

“That’s what I hear,” Lois said.

Randy added warm-blooded facts to his notebook.

He spotted
Orson the owl.

"A mammal?"
"*Hoo, boy*. Not me. Most
mammals don't have wings."

"So, mammals can't fly?" Randy asked.

"Oh, there's one that can. But mostly, only birds and insects can fly."

Randy saw Stella the stick bug.

"Are you a mammal?" Randy asked.
Stella stopped crawling.
"A mammal?" she said. "Seriously?
Mammals have no more than four limbs.
How many do I have?"
Randy counted. "Looks like six?" he said.
"Most mammals use all four limbs to
move around," Stella said.
"Even baby humans!"

Randy made another note.

It was getting late. Randy saw Brady the bat. "Hey, wait a second!" Randy called.

The little rat guessed Brady probably wasn't. Brady could fly like a bird. Birds weren't mammals.

"Yes I am!" Brady called back.
"I'm the only mammal that can fly."

"My first mammal!"

Brady grabbed Randy and flew away. Where was Brady taking him?

When they landed, Randy saw a bunch of animals. They had hair. They had four limbs. Randy looked at his own hairy body. He fit right in! He was a mammal, too!

"Are you all mammals?"

"Yes," Roxy the raccoon said happily. "And you are too!"

"I know," Randy said.

MAMMAL MEET-UP

Randy's Notebook

MAMMALS . . .

- Are born "alive." They do not hatch from eggs.
  Well... except for platypuses and echidnas.
- Feed their babies milk from the mother.
- Take care of their babies. They teach them survival skills.
- Have fur or hair.
- Are warm-blooded.
- Have four limbs to move around. Even humans, when they're babies.
- Cannot fly, except for bats! Bats are
  the only mammals with wings.

GLOSSARY

cold-blooded Having a body temperature that changes to match the surrounding temperature.

fur The coat of thick, soft hair on the skin of an animal.

insect A small animal with six legs, three parts to its body, and a hard outer skeleton.

limb A part of a body used in moving or grasping, such as arms, legs, flippers, or wings.

warm-blooded Having a body temperature that stays about the same no matter what the air temperature is.

WEBSITES

BioKids—Kids' Inquiry of Diverse Species—Mammals

http://www.biokids.umich.edu/critters/Mammalia/

Mammals: National Geographic Kids

https://kids.nationalgeographic.com/animals/mammals

Mammals | San Diego Zoo Animals and Plants

https://animals.sandiegozoo.org/animals/mammals

READ MORE

Drimmer, Stephanie Warren. *Ultimate Mammalpedia.* Washington, D.C.: National Geographic Kids, 2023.

Gunasekara, Mignonne & Charis Mather. *Mighty Mammals.* Minneapolis: Bearport Publishing Company, 2024.

Owen, Ruth. *Animal Classification.* Minneapolis: Bearport Publishing Company, 2024.

AMICUS ILLUSTRATED is published by
Amicus Learning, an imprint of Amicus
P.O. Box 227, Mankato, MN 56002
www.amicuspublishing.us

Library of Congress Cataloging-in-Publication Data
Names: Troupe, Thomas Kingsley, author. | Rotondo, Martina, illustrator.
Title: Are you a mammal? / by Thomas Kingsley Troupe ; illustrated by Martina Rotondo.
Description: Mankato, MN : Amicus Illustrated, [2025] | Series: Animal classification | Includes bibliographical references. | Audience: Ages 6–9 | Audience: Grades 2–3 | Summary: "When young Randy the rat overhears Forrest the frog grumbling about mammals, Randy sets out on a mission to find out what exactly a mammal is. After interviewing other animals in the forest and learning about the characteristics of mammals, Randy realizes that he too is a mammal! Includes fact page, glossary, and resources for further research"— Provided by publisher.
Identifiers: LCCN 2024010604 (print) | LCCN 2024010605 (ebook) | ISBN 9798892001175 (library binding) | ISBN 9798892001755 (paperback) | ISBN 9798892002332 (ebook)
Subjects: LCSH: Mammals—Juvenile literature. | Mammals—Classification—Juvenile literature. | Animals—Classification—Juvenile literature.
Classification: LCC QL706.2 .T76 2025 (print) | LCC QL706.2 (ebook) | DDC 599.01/2—dc23/eng/20240405
LC record available at https://lccn.loc.gov/2024010604
LC ebook record available at https://lccn.loc.gov/2024010605

Printed in China

Editor: Rebecca Glaser
Designer: Kim Pfeffer

ABOUT THE AUTHOR

Thomas Kingsley Troupe is the author of more than 200 books for young readers. When he's not writing, he enjoys reading, playing video games, and investigating haunted places with the Twin Cities Paranormal Society. Otherwise, he's probably taking a nap or something. Thomas lives in Woodbury, Minnesota with his two sons.

ABOUT THE ILLUSTRATOR

Artist since always, Martina Rotondo attended the Master of Illustration and Concept Art at The Sign Academy in Florence, Italy. She currently works as an illustrator for both Italian and foreign publishing houses. Lover of traditional drawing, she is also constantly researching and experimenting with new techniques to create her surreal and engaging characters and backgrounds.

ARE YOU A . . . ?